EXIΔNA

ECHIDNA

or

The Many Adventures of
HINENĀKAHIRUA *as She Tries to Find*
Her Place in a Colonised World

included throughout is the story of MĀUI-PŌTIKI & PROMETHEUS

essa may ranapiri

TE HERENGA WAKA
UNIVERSITY PRESS

Te Herenga Waka University Press
Victoria University of Wellington
PO Box 600 Wellington
teherengawakapress.co.nz

First published 2022
Reprinted 2022

A catalogue record is available at the National Library of New Zealand

ISBN 9781776920099

Printed in Aotearoa New Zealand by Ligare

for my ancestors / for my descendants

CONTENTS

IV

V

VI

VII

Dramatis Personae | He Tāngata

Echidna: eponymous character, Greek Mother of Monsters & messy takatāpui wahine. Has two long snake tails instead of legs. (she/they)

Adam: the first man according to Genesis, is a dummy. (he/him)

a figure that sits on the other side of the water: a person that lives alone in a tower. (they/ia)

Argus Panoptes: a creature with many eyes. (he/him)

Christian dad: is a dad and is also Christian, left a while back. (he/him)

Elon Musk: sent a car into space as a show of power. (he/him)

Eve (1): the first woman according to Genesis. (she/her)

Eve (2): a person that Echidna likes hanging out with. (she/they/he)

Gaia: embodiment of nature. (she/her)

Gerard Way: singer of the band My Chemical Romance. (he/they)

Hatupatu AKA The Te Arawa boy: enough about him already. (he/him)

Hemi: a Māori boy who found himself in England. (he/him)

Herculine: a real person who was murdered by the state for being intersex, please look her up. Rest in power. (she/her)

Hinemoa: a swimmer. (she/ia)

Hine-nui-te-pō: the atua of death, cares a lot, too much maybe. (she/her)

Hineraukatauri: Gay with moth wings. (she/her)

Jeff Bezos: when not if. (he/him)

Jesus: yeah that one. (he/him)

Judas: a traitor or *the* traitor (he/him)

Kronos: leader of the Titans, apparently doesn't understand the difference between babies and rocks. (he/him)

Kurangaituku: the Bird-woman. A kaiako. (she/her)

Lucifer: a fallen angel, commonly known as the Devil. (xe/xir)

Māhinaarangi: drew her love to her with the perfume of the Raukawa tree. (she/ia)

Mahuika: the atua of fire. Had no eyes. (she/her)

Mauao: a sad boy maunga. (he/him)

Māui-Pōtiki: a trickster who has a fraught relationship with death. (he/him)

Michael: an angel, annoying. (xe/xyr)

Milton: an old poet, was blind and hated the monarchy. (he/him)

Nafanua: a Samoan warrior goddess. (she/her)

Narcissus: a person with a great interest in reflection. (they/them)

Papatūānuku: the earth, te ao. (she/ia)

Pipi: a drag queen named. (she/her)

Poūkahangatus: revolutionary wahine Māori, a gorgon. (she/her)

Prometheus: a Titan that has an interest in fire. (he/they)

Punga: atua of the ugly things. (he/him)

Rehua: of the stars, knows a lot of stuff. (he/him)

Rona: a person with a fraught relationship with the moon. Echidna likes them, like, like-likes them. (they/she/he)

Sisyphus: apparently stuck doing the same task forever, we know the truth. (they/them)

Tamanuiterā: the sun boy. (he/him)

Tāne Mahuta: atua of the ngahere. (he/him)

Tangaroa: atua of the sea. (he/him)

Tū-te-wehiwehi: the father of all reptiles, one of Echidna's dads. (ia)

The Drone: a drone. Working class and violent. (she/her)

The Last Moahunter: someone from a long time ago. (ia)

The Sirens: musicians who live in the sea. (she/her)

The Spider: takatāpui wahine, the coolest bish around. (she/her)

Tāwhirimātea: atua of the wind. In a blind rage. (he/ia)

Tiki: a Te Arawa ancestor. (he/ia)

Tūmatauenga: atua of war, also of People. (he/him)

Tūtānekai: ancestor with bi energy. (he/ia)

Typhon: the Father of Monsters, mostly absent from this book. A good lay. (he/him)

Uenuku: atua of the rainbow, living in a carving at Te Awamutu museum. (any pronouns with respect)

Un-named Snake Woman: only a snake would care for her own. (she/her)

Ureia: a taniwha. (they/them)

Wikitoria AKA Victoria: a dead queen. (she/her)

Zoa: two-spirit Oji-cree, also a cyborg with a soul of glitter. (he/him)

She-viper with Tales Outstretched

Sculpture by Pirro Ligorio, 1555

after torrin a. greathouse's 'Medusa with the Head of Perseus'

1. What begins to be by spreading?
    Is she a mother is she a mother is she a mother
    of monsters in a field of monsters?
    What hot summer is a snake doing in New Zealand?
    What cruise ship or container ship did she make it here on?
    Or was she a swimmer like Hinemoa? Or has she been here since
    the first voyages?

2. What decade is the worst to go through puberty for a trans girl?
    She lived through many of them. Her body spiralling outwards.
    She gets to choose the second one and the third.

3. Echidna is a dangerous animal; she pokes holes in men just to
    remind them what kind of monster she is wakes up every single
    morning and chooses violence cos what choice does she really have?

4. Her gigantic statued form still stands in Sacro Bosco. One of the
    only times she's seen herself and not flinched. Let the stonework
    inspire fear. Let it make grown men quiver, tongues dry; *If I were to
    be crushed by this beast, I would be thankful.*

5. She fucks with stories and storytelling even more so when they're
    not about her, how unfortunate; this book.

6. Does she miss everyone she's loved? Or do they hang from headphone cords tangled inside her liver? Do they hold onto their own little crosses and whisper to God for her?

7. How many times has she died and how many times will she come back, her name changed her body more monstrous? Hinenākahirua looks back at Echidna's life; where does one stop and the other really begin?

I

A SNAKE SLITHERS
THROUGH THE GRASS

an egg cracks open
in the ocean
and
something
comes out

Echidna: Born of Eve & Lucifer

they meet underneath the apples   on the sabbath to fuck in the bushes
she couldn't help but love   when the forked tongue made an electric feast
of her soft flesh   such a division she never felt while being another
man's rib   she knows all the scales in the world   and knows the
snake is   a liar   but why shouldn't she be able to have some fun
while it lasts   and Adam is as thick as a post anyway   always finishing
too fast   with Adam   she was   a way for the first man to jack
himself off   the serpent   cared about her   pleasure
at least   the ferns bob as if a current has passed through them

The Snake Woman

for Roma Potiki

Echidna cries in the meadow
all raw gums and grabby hands
scales chaffing softly
          softly away

another snake
woman   enters the garden
all the ground folded   hands gone dry

a drummer hitting the high hat
    as she swaddles the babe
splashing sound on   dead land
    as she swaddles the babe
in flax
fingers gone waxy and curl

they both go   in the river
mineral dance   at their entrance
gargle of rushing   whimper of calming

where does the hot water take them?

Echidna & Uenuku

As a toddler she plays with stones.

Finds the ones full to the brim with rainbow.

And sucks on them like hardboiled eggs.

Echidna & Her Brothers

when they play chase round the back
of the house   beige paint peeling from
the weatherboard   she is always the
taniwha   by virtue of her tails   she figures
that it's fair that way
Echidna and her brothers all dressed in hand-me-down
shirts with holes ratting the hems
run round the house making an entire field out of an
urban backyard
but they're too quick   with their legs
growing longer   she is indebted to a slither
has to master a difficult traction
they're too far ahead so
the game moves from tag to hide-and-seek
she looks   behind a rock   where one brother is
squashing mum's hydrangeas   and looks up to see
another is wrapped bodily   around a branch

when it's her turn she hides in the laundry   next to the
ghastly growl of the washing machine   as it turns

Echidna & Her Christian Dad

went to church every Sunday until work got too hectic the cross warm from how he would press it into his palm make up for all the absence he thought it would make up for everything he thought Echidna had taken to gardening around this time pulling long weeds like green veins from the soil turn it over with trowel to dig a space for horopito and pikopiko the tomatoes already fat bulbs red boils hanging from the stalk ready to pop her mother tells her to be careful of her body   not to crush the plants   afterwards she's picking dirt from underneath her fingernails lingering on that watered-down-coffee-grind smell she would pray for her father to get home early she would read the first page of the bible repeatedly watch God create he would make it to the sixth day start again and be so happy with what He had done and start again would make mankind in His own image start again Echidna reckoned he must look beastly a God with 14 billion eyes to see everyone and everything start – gets caught on *subdue the earth* feels sad in a way she can't explain – again fingers the fibrous page so easy to rip for something so important she prays that her father gets home early without the Old Testament rage and hunger of the Israelites it takes three hours to prepare briam *in the beginning* she prays she hasn't started too late puts tomatoes in the pan with onions to make it sauce

Echidna Meets Hine-nui-te-pō

she's unsure how long chocolate will last in this heat   imagining it melting to
sugary mud in its golden wrappers   fundraising for her trip overseas   *it would*
mean a lot   it's that time of the year   *no thank you no thank you no thank you*
they didn't like the look of her   thought the neighbourhood would be a bad
idea   obviously made of money   but money doesn't give to little brown girls
with tails   she knocks   on a door painted black or burnt black   she is not
sure   she has lost count of how many times she has knocked   it opens   an
old Māori woman with long white hair   peppered with pits of black   *Kia*
ora kōtiro   she's wearing a long cloak made of feathers   her moko
kauae moves as she speaks   hugging the bottom of her lip   like blood
long dried   *Kia ora kuia*   she's lost her script   *here to fundraise*   she
manages it out somehow   *What's your name dear?*   Echidna replies   her
name feels like a wager as it leaves her mouth   she splutters *but you could call*
me Hinenākahirua   *What a beautiful name*   she bends down
come here love and presses her nose to Echidna's   there is death inside of the
breath somehow   dark eyes staring intent   *here*   and coins are
dripping into the box   she removes two blocks   *Would you like to come*
inside? don't get many visitors as bright eyed as you, got the kettle on   she spies
the woman's necklace all obsidian   black shark's teeth or tear drops   she
doesn't know what to say   but gestures at her box of chocolates   tries to
form the phrase *A lot of houses to go*   fails but   Hine-nui-te-pō just nods
understanding   Echidna leaves with the question hanging   in the air

Māui & Prometheus Have a Meet-cute

it's not that pottery scene from *Ghost*
or the sweaty handprint on glass in *Titanic*

it's nothing like the leaf-pulped perfume of Māhinaarangi
or the slow silent letting go of Tiki and Tūtānekai

it's not dropping books in the hall and stumbling
in sync to pick them up
it's not asking someone out at lunch twice to two
different responses
a *yes* and then
a *no*
sandwiches weeping inside gladwrap

or dancing silently at the end of things
how shoes scuff across polished floors
and throw up light and shadow
nothing so romantic as dinner or a picnic
pocket lint in uncut grass

it's a small text in the late hours
Prometheus asking *are you attracted to me*
and Māui responding
yes
you took long enough to catch on

II

SHE GROWS INTO AND OUT OF THINGS THAT STICK

There is always something
awkward
about growing up.
A single hair growing out from a mole
pointing in the wrong direction.

Echidna Goes through Her Emo Phase

she sits on her bed   the lamp propped up   on copies of R.S. Thomas &
Milton's epic   a warm glow to give her sight enough   *The Art of*
Drowning playing on her Walkman   hand hovered over the   pause button
she's writing out the lyrics   one line at a time   her best guess 'mystical as
purring animals' crawls into her heart where it folds   itself into the bed
of its pump   she wipes her eyes free of sleep smudging mascara   she isn't
used to applying   puts holes through her sleeves to tuck thumbs
through the gap   stabs a poster of Gerard Way onto the wall   and asks
for him to wait for her   like that would somehow slow down the age gap

standing in the shower now she scrubs vivid from her tails   kids' comics
and lyrics   from the radio   Black Parade and a Riot! of melodrama   when
she gets out   lifting her unruly form over the threshold   she wraps clichés
around herself to get dry   the mirror fogged over   hides a reflection she
doesn't see herself in

Echidna & Her Own Image

all around her are paintings of an old   white man trying to eat his son
varying stages of consumption   and levels of dress

that gentle tug on the boy's breast   giving way to Goya's headless gore

all these careful representations   implicating whiteness into power
so many brush strokes   for that dead god's ego
she sees none of herself   her picture hides on the internet   on
DeviantArt and Tumblr where her eyes become a cartoon   of sight

adjacent to pornography   the whore   the beast   the same
she wonders if her great-grandfather Punga   would appreciate people
finding beauty in   ugliness
she shakes her head these men   obviously had a thing for vore
or else   why bother?

under her tongue she finds the oil   paint so dry and spits until it runs
a mouth gone   into a red waterfall

Echidna Meets Another Eve

for Aimee-Jane Anderson-O'Connor

chimeric in the last light of the day Echidna watches Eve   squish sandwiches
into tupperware   the crusts folding upwards to form two long brown strips
the idea of lips   spread thin   *do I know you* she asks pushing the lid down
Echidna standing in the doorway brushing the linoleum   doesn't have words
for what she wants to say but just nods   *like from a long time ago?*
Echidna smiles *something like that* Eve places the container in her schoolbag
Athletics day tomorrow   scrunches folded PE gear into the main pocket
Echidna smiles at that   *my favourite is shotput I imagine the people in the*
field and aim for where they are standing   Echidna raises both her
eyebrows   *the shot never lands just thuds right on through* Eve explains
away the violence   but Echidna knows   it didn't start   with
her

Echidna in Kirikiriroa over the Summer

wades through shallows of the Waikato   not really clean enough to be a
part of   doesn't remember how to talk to the river   despite their
personhood

fills a VR booth at Timeout   killing imaginary things with imaginary
weaponry   pixels splattered apart   the whole time she can't
escape worries about how she is seen   in the world   does she deserve the
leisure afforded her   leaves without spending the roll of tokens

at Browsers she lies serpentine   to check out NZ poetry
the shelf for verse hugs the floor   pages sick and yellow

ute drives to town with her and two others under tarpaulin   they hang out
stationary in the Backbar while she shakes through her depression
snakedance into the night   sees her ex on the way home   Echidna tries
her best to ignore   the flush red   and the eyes like blue drops of water frozen
into ice   but   says hi   so unfortunately   straw hair stuck to
the side of her face with sweat   Echidna shakes out her dark curls   in
response   smirks waves   but feels black in the pit of her

there is a hole in the Ozone directly above the city   the future of the sky
the future of the sun   she welcomes the warmth for her blood   Tamanuiterā
hasn't felt so close in so long   Echidna still gets so cold at night   was
she supposed to be good at holding the heat in by now   sees Rona cradled in
the moon   hard to balance what the body wants with what the body
needs

she's the best at beerpong but only after getting a few away   needs drunk-
bright light   the ball plopped in those red cups everyone buys from the
Warehouse   orders chicken burgers from Hillcrest Fastfoods   eyes the
smorgasbord   would save her the weird looks if she didn't have to wait for her
order   but she waits   it's routine

thinks about camping at Raglan for the new year   whose new year is it really?
misses her koro   the ocean   as far as it gets where she is at   or could she
go east and see her pākehā family   Christmas-weirdness
huddles around poor Mauao giving him stale headlines and quiet judgement
she has to sit with people she loves and swallow racist barbs   *we*
don't get what you've become   no real maa-rees left anyway   all evil
stems from Zespri or the Indians stealing our orchards   Echidna feels
monstrous at the table for lunch   next to that chill infection   feels like
all evil stems from her

Echidna & Her Bird Tongue

for Gem Wilder

it starts with the sound of birds
when she is barely awake
the world reminding her it's there
in the best way possible

Papatūānuku reaching into her dreams
and laying her bare
it is so simple

just listen!   we got our language from
feathers and flight
just listen
we got our language from the nests in the
trees

Kurangaituku flying backwards
out of the geothermal pools
completely intact
ready to teach that boy Hatupatu
how to put together a sentence

Echidna Gets a Name Change

at the age of 19 she doesn't really feel like a mum
not ready to be all split open and building an army
between her navel and her scales
feels pōhara about where it comes from versus where she
came from
before she can save the money to make it official
one-hundred-and-fifty-fucking-dollars
she gets her friends to call her Hinenākahirua
she don't want to be white-washed by the classics no more
she is a daughter of te ao Māori   & proud!

her friends are cool with it
the Olympians are not
think about everyone who will struggle
with the syllables
don't want to be putting knots in human tongues
guilt trip on a slipstream Kronos stuffing rocks in his gob

she gets self-conscious then
maybe she hasn't earned a Māori name
maybe she won't fit in with it anyways
a second thought piled on second thoughts

WINZ cuts her payment when they find out
about her moonlighting at the meatworks
makes the decision for her
Echidna remains Echidna in name alone

Echidna & Her Life

when she puts the point
to the hard parts of her
they slough away like fish flakes
the blade comes back bloodless
like a carving she has no choice in shaping
& she feels
ashamed

Māui-Pōtiki & Prometheus Make Love on Mt Elbrus

after June Gehringer's 'Prometheus as queer icon'

beak and fingers clash
Māui as hawk   as eagle
as anything Prometheus wants him to be
and all amount of swallowing   *I could live*
on this one says   pulling at the ate   neither sure it doesn't leave
their own lips   two bodies as open entrances   him in him
in him   find embers in the centre *never flown*
like this before   never fucked in feathers
Māui holds back the sun   to make the night
last longer and longer   he places the hook
in Prometheus's mouth   feels solid and melting
tips riddled with flame they tuha together
make the rock hot   with fluids
crowning Elbrus in waitātea

III

REVOLUTIONARY
PARTY MONSTER

dance
dance
dance
dance
kill

Echidna Goes Out on the Town; Meets Typhon

she's got the fattest green stone
around her neck to complement
her scales   her scars thicker than most; electric white
branches across her back, a sea of crackle smoothed black
she's all envy when it comes to shoes all envy
but her moves are slick as shit   leaves a trail of Corona
plinking in the gutter   how many tears in the glass
from paper hearts to rip up   the dance floor and leave em

she sees him chugging DBs a cut on his cheek
got that Tūmatauenga swagger   the fist so naturally formed
a face only a mother could love   teeth broken fifty fifty all stained
gorgeous crinkling in leather
he gives Echidna the once over
mofo with eyes like the spark   gets her giddy
she knocks him one in the gullet   a distinct crack in reciprocation
flash of reverence   ice-hella-broke
they get to words   he whakapapas from old Gaia
hails from Ischia   all gauze yellow gauze green
them wairua echoes   or just looking for a good lay
continue to drink till the moon is fat
bigger than she expects after his talk of size
they go off together   shed skins in the bushes
next to the highway

Echidna & Narcissus

for jayy dodd

Echidna & Narcissus run through the forest

in Tāne's forest none of the trees cat-call they all
come silently for new life in the leaves
leaves them all alone as they run through the dusk
everyone has an understanding here the panopticon
is made of kindness the way eyes move across
skin and weigh each pigment in a scale
but a ghost to be left screaming in the sun
Narcissus is chasing a dark reflection through the trees
in the depths they hold hands as they skip in
Tāne's forest can feel a million daughters rushing with them

Echidna & Narcissus in an apartment building

do i look like a question mark / to u they ask sitting with a clock
between their legs / Echidna thinks what a thing to be
the punctuation that throws / everything into wonder

Echidna & Narcissus at the river

they're staring at the surface eyes looking past themselves
Echidna is reaching out to make a ripple
Narcissus: *i didn't think you were gonna be that bold*
to rip the river's face
Echidna responds with: *it is only my face disturbed*
Narcissus just laughs trying to figure out who they are in the current
this is what i call transitioning can you see it
Echidna can
i think u love the river so because all ur ancestors' souls move through it
Narcissus makes themselves into a straight line
i can see their black bodies fly through the darkness of the rip
i can see them without shame
without the tattered roles of gender in their moving
Echidna feels tears well up
the river making its way out of her face
in here i can be whoever the fuck i am

Echidna Dances w/ Poūkahangatus & All the Colours of the Wind

for Tayi Tibble

wāhine of the wage gap   queens of inequality   wrist watches with a plastic
glint   products   of a racist system   Echidna watches
Poūkahangatus dance in the club
she's activist black panther with snakes running out the cap
tresses all glisten back to bark   they share that scale   north and south
share the house of the basilisk   see those bougie politicians all carved into
works of art   she grinding up on frozen foible

they work the floor like experts   working a flaw out of the body at night
shoes suctioning to the schlop of the rtd-stick
Echidna has never felt the solidarity   she feels sweating out all the fucks
she's weighed down by   a hope that they can make it   all bright poise
and shimmer

poison Bezos with his crown all marble shine
a newspaper caricature   with added weight

Echidna Starts an Instagram Account

#freak on her first selfie
let them think what they will
she's holding the light in her mouth
and swallowing the world
make fetish out of queerness and sell it wholesale
shaking tails in a still frame
her story so many pips to keep the interest up
she whakapapas to storytellers
daddy day by daddy day
put it in a filter
Echidna is the baddest of bitches
chasers only good as the money they give
don't have to love dogs if he owns a beachside apartment
and she can stay on weekends or any day she wants

she got them lizard men market cornered

One Must Imagine Sisyphus Is Actually Doing Something Incredibly Important

for Hana Pera Aoake

they are rolling   it around the lowest cave system
pushing this one   boulder   up and up
and up   from below   u can see them
hustling for something   called eternity
it rolls and rolls and rolls and rolls and rolls and rolls and rolls
and rolls and rolls and rolls and rolls and rolls and rolls and rolls . . .
can see them make a difference   with every single rotation
as the boulder gains   mass   more and more and more
as they roll it   rolls and rolls and rolls
and the story gathers   steam oh
look it's ole Sisyphus   ole getting-nothing-done
rolls and rolls and rolls and rolls and rolls and rolls
rolls and rolls and rolls and rolls and rolls and rolls and . . .
how quick the rest forget   how much Sisyphus had already
accomplished   how quick to underestimate
the change that   a big rock dropped from a great height
can facilitate   once you've already stolen immortality
from the gods   then revolution should come easy

Echidna & Nafanua

for Tusiata Avia

the whole world inside
the jacket of a mince pie
fresh out of the microwave

one is lying on the couch   the other is sizzling out on the deck
all UV ray red.   the sliding door ajar   C4 pumping
through the top 20   808 drum machines   and autotune
and edgy   eyeliner   vocalists
all pronouncement all gusto   and head voice
neither is really listening   to what is going on
spilled orange   citric clots to the little wooden table
propped up by wrappers and   discarded paper

so many poems that   neither gives a shit about now the sun has
hit the land   eels wrapping themselves around snakes with straining jaws
just passing each other in the light
what are warrior women gonna do between   battles
except enjoy the summers   as they enjoy them now
that they   won't last

Mahuika & Prometheus Discuss the Pros + Cons of Fire

flicker   it's a light   inside rock
the star   that the iris will seize

and expands out to the size of an open space   at night
eats wood without   asking if it is   consumes land
and controls   life   put the mechanism   inside a mine   napalm
held in the hand   of an animal   to make space
for civilisation   and its hunger

pale flame to spread empire
makes all manner of machines
to move the sky full of it

it brings food out of flesh   and warmth
with which to survive the night
and that night can be so much longer than

longer than what

birds flying through

longer than you thought

Māui hears none of this   his aunt distracted   he steals
her fingernails   and runs off with his very own petal of sun

IV

TRICKLE DOWN
COLONISATION
&
A WORLD TOUR

Is it a cliché
to use the big ol c word
or is it irresponsible to
ignore
the fences cut across the land?

Echidna Tries Her Best to Console Herculine

for Aaron Apps

Echidna tries to stretch herself over the silence   of not understanding
here in Wīwī   they find an intimacy   called alone   combat an ennui   made
of state control   does death make things better in the books   Herculine
is already shaking   Echidna turns towards them   holds the back of
Herculine's head like an egg she's scared of cracking   they meet at the nose
Echidna can feel the hair growing like fingers on Herculine's upper lip   the
physicians tell her it is wrong   Echidna isn't sure that's even the right way of
looking at it   they sit like this for a while breathing each other in

the stove turned off at the wall

Echidna & Her Milton

thumbs through pages of misprint after mis
print of *Paradise Lost*   in awe at the
heavens they hold pressed   into leaves are plants
ferns and seeds from a   place she calls home her
whenua trapped   in the imaginat
-ion of an   Englishman all Technicol-
or glass and   gaudy relief genderless
angels working   for a greater power
no   matter   how   against   the   monarchy
he was   the irony   stains   her fingers

Echidna & Hemi in Rānana

for Tina Makereti

they're both festival attractions in their own right   such a shocking character
such epic shadows   for them whities to paint an image onto but they are
both writers   too fully capable   of spilling their
own   narrative   Echidna hates   it here   in the belly of
          the beast away   from her   whenua
Hemi tells her he thinks this   is hell and heaven   squashed   and
Echidna just blinks it would   be the saddest   thing to die under the
gaze of Wikitoria who wears   black some mock   grief costume is she
feeling sorry for herself when   all the empire is   hers? Hemi winces
and looks down at his feet trying   to imagine   them sinking into
mud trying to imagine a different   kind of world in be
tween his toes the smell is a wretched thing the Thames so thoroughly decayed

Echidna & Ureia

for Carin Smeaton

i.

she's smiling the whole time
as they swim Tīkapa
brushing up against the churn of ocean
on the rocks
the waves folding over and under their bodies
Tangaroa tugging at their feet
drawing them out
then pushing them back in
playing rush against the pebbles
skimming them across
the mirror of the sky
another serpent
completely unlike her so completely at home
here
watches Ureia move their awesome size
through the currents

ii.

they are selling parcels of Ureia's flesh
twenty-five dollars a pound
each pound a punch
in the stomach

she goes to them lying still in the moana
and asks to hold them
Ureia nods weakly
she runs her fingers along
the taniwha's teeth
thinking about games of tag
thinking of games without
the same repercussions as this
the shell jagged
softened
runs her fingers over the barnacles that still cling
around the holes they put in Ureia's flesh
the great big cuts
still gushing bloody into the water
Echidna can feel the pain
know its bite in her own serpent nature
long calls to the heavens
that stretch
Ureia to sleep

iii.

Echidna is first
pleased   then horrified to see
them again
standing in the Auckland War Memorial Museum
how could they hold u here?
she touches the rākau and feels them try
their best to touch back

a feeling that sits inside her
for years afterwards

Echidna Is a Cleaner at Night

for Miri

bleach stings in the wrinkles   of her knuckles as she's blasting the shit
off the walls   the muscle stench   the kaimoana clung too long
inland   she's thinking about her workmates and getting drunk
on the weekend   *is it Friday yet?*   the soft giving up of flesh
unprickling itself   unwrapped velcro swell

the black dye   that wets the nightened cement
the season is running out   the wet kraken drip
draining into the gutters   slopping through the grates

she's pushing the trolley   full of things to clean the world with
and she wears a smile that   carries all her ancestors through the good
and the bad of an afterlife   held under the union jack and some token stars

Echidna Goes to See the Drone Perform in Front of a Live Audience

after Harry Josephine Giles's 'Drone'

Echidna sits in the crowd while the drone hums her song in the air
watches as she just hangs there
in glitter shine w/ two layers of lipstick
suspended on blades that spin and spin and spin

it is a drone making a droooone
noise   the notes are waterfalling to spit against the ground

the drone shares a story in the splash
about her cat
about being a woman with a dick that hangs limp between her drone legs
        (nervous at a party   talking to some militarised version
                of Argus Panoptes
                        alllllll of the eyes are watching)
about her job experience
about the violence inherent
or inherited in the
experience of   of   of   of

there are bees in the slideshow behind her
worker bees in a colony

the drone that is a pun   or a punishing tonic   to   the rhetoric of sale of
selling of buying of   of of of of

Echidna can't help but cry as the drone places her own head
in the filing cabinet
as the drone prays for a quiet death at home

not a falling apart inside any number of her targets

Echidna wonders if the pot-plant is in there too? the filing cabinet
she can't quite remember
that fragile lick of nature   of something we made of something they made us do

buying out selling out out out out   there

Echidna is inside the panopticon   trying to reach out and save the drone
from her preprogrammed cycle   the whirr that won't stop

the pātere that stretches between
her the drone and
her the mother of monsters
is nothing like the orders either is used to
the doctrine of divide and subtract
of work yourself to the bone
the carbon-fibre frame trembling
in wire network fizz

where they both hold onto either end of the string
the porotiti spins and disrupts the air
as they step into a different world
moving hands towards each other and back
coil and uncoil
flinging air in a way
that catches the tragedy of the situation
in the husk of the laughter that bumps against the stage lights

Echidna Asks Rona One Hundred Questions

for Reihana Robinson

Echidna traces the paths   that they must have taken
finds where the tree had been   Rona moving between genders
at the whim of   whoever delivers the story   from whenua to whenua
Echidna feels a kinship here   plucking dags of dirt out of the ngaio
pulled up   through some magic   to find herself with the
man not-man not-woman in the moon

Echidna sees Rona's long white hair   and his long white nails as a sign
there is mana in the way Rona holds herself   an orb of light
Echidna pours questions into the quiet
*did you get enough water?   fill up the gourd to cry a stream from that
coin in the air?   do you still have the roots?   could you fold my
umbilical into those dry fingers?*   Rona just stares   how eyes look when
they hold   more than what can be seen
*did you flee the earth or were you taken?   what did we bury inside your
name?   were you a woman eaten by the moon?   or a moon eaten by a man?   or
was everything mixed up? and mixed in?*
Rona turns   first one way then the other   before saying *I can't quite
grasp the solidness of the satellite   it all runs away from me here*

after a long silence Echidna asks

would you run away with me here?

the silence after is something they both fall into

Prometheus & His Lover's Great Accomplishment

for Sam Duckor-Jones

Prometheus is in the garage moulding
little men into being
fingers slick with clay
drying gradually into dust
the light casts shadows to move
the roller door open to let the air in

a breeze meanders from tool to tool
breathes against all the fishing rods
his lover has hung from the wall

Māui has caught some big ones
in his day

he sits his tiny figure up on the shelf
with the others
he can see it on their faces
(scrunched fingernail detailing)
they all want something
he isn't sure he's allowed to give

could he be as brave to draw a world
over the horizon against its will?

V

ECHIDNA GIVES THE
STAGE UP TO OTHERS
BECAUSE THAT'S JUST
HOW HUMBLE SHE IS

Kāore te kūmara
e kōrero mō tōna
ake reka.

Does this joke
translate?

Hineraukatauri & Her Lover

for Ruby Solly

she stands up on her balcony flute at the crook of her lips   her great moth
wings gently brushing against the paint peel and lichen   her partner has
their guitar   rested on their leg strumming along
open chords in the open air

she remembers back   to the whare tapere
where she learned to play   where their eyes met   as they danced through
movements of the poi
                back to the Denny's where they shared
Grilled Cheese and the Super Bird Sandwich with a healthy side of fries   a
melody of its own drifting up into the extraction fan   the salt and fat
what else would you cook love in

back to the call of the moa in the night   that deep throated bass
note warbling   she would go   and touch the sides   of   the
great bird   its rumble calm beneath her fingers   its feathers   like
a kind of fur   but importantly   not

     the distance that sound travels   man   the distance
through the thickness of history books   their linear patterns   and
paper cuts   travelling through   white lies   until all that's left
are *did-you-knows* in the small hours   the periphery   of some grand
warfare   nothing fair dates tumbling out   under duvets

   till she's standing there on the deck   in Rātana colours   cocoons
unfolding all around her   the soft christening of an old life crunching open
singing across Aro Valley   guitar plucking all the while

Zoa

for Joshua Whitehead

: : ::::: : rorohiko hustle data thru ::::::: ::: : th wildebeest of mbs : : :::: a fan
spinning itself to death :::: :: : inside :: : : th machine : : : : a rat stuck in a steel
box : : ::: a blowtorch humming it red : :::: : Zoa is reclined on a receipt of : : ::
food is too expensive to : : ::: live on : : once again : : : ::: he's resting his feet on th
::::: arm of the couch : : ::: dreaming of motorbikes travelling over th great plains :
: :: a cloud of Pōpokotea : :: : : : : caping out behind him :::::::: : what spirit is not
doubled :: double double doublehelix : : : :: here in this wairua! : : :::: here in this
place where rivers cross their streams : :: : : double double doublehelix :::: there can
be a willing and whiling :: : & th spinning : : : dust devil :::: try it :: Zoa got : : :
:: : : th magic :: : : collage :: an engorged penis over the ::: union jack and : : be
done with it ::: to blow those fucking : : : white. slave. owning. rapists. :: right off
the ::: face of maunga so many-spirited :: you'd think all the ancestors showed up
: : ::: to cuss them out

Mauao & the Angel Michael

he sits there   eyes glued on the moana   *look at it move*
look at it rush   oh how drowning   would feel so much better
than this   what size   he has become   in this stillness
and he doesn't want to look at   whoever is hovering there
praying for his eternal soul   a bird the shape of a man
or a woman   or somewhere non-specific
you will soon be able to move   i swear
xe says in a voice more grating
than any bird Mauao   has ever heard
waving around a needle   made of fire   that Michael calls
freedom   grimaces at the reminder   if he still had it in him
he would have   blown his top   and turned the birdboi
into so much   ash and   cinder   but he just stands there
endlessly unavailable   endlessly about to
jump   the sun constantly
talking him down   back from the edge
the shadow he casts behind himself
makes a negative of all the space
that is defined as *him*
but still Michael refuses
to keep xir prayers to xirself
while Mauao knows all too well
the nature of
an eternal soul
built out of rock
as he is

Tūmatauenga at the Frontlines

wtf   some white man served by   this
should have let   Tāwhirimātea have his
fucking way with the Bros   to end up
here on the other side   of the planet
blowing away   people he has no
connection to   except for the violence
told by some imperial state   the civilian
populace must   pay their utu   while
the drone performs   her sound   and fury
over the distant   horizon   Tamanuiterā
bleeding over the landscape   like a soldier
that just won't die   *how much is there inside*
you to spill   cuz   Tū watches
the men he serves with   tear
through their enemies   knives
through wet tissue   just a target to be
punctured   NZ Army's hollow haka for
Ngāti Boot-licker   their simulacrum
of the warrior   Tū spits   into the dirt
of all that noble savage   all that warrior gene
while they shine leather soles with their pūkana
nothing noble in a hollow point   nothing
genetic about having   your community
destroyed   by some fuckers with a big book
he even answers to Tū now   *just Tū*
hoping it's   short enough   *that those eggs*
won't have the time to pin   all these crimes
                        to his name

Hinemoana

for Elizabeth, Sinead, Michelle & Hinemoana

Hinemoana reads poetry in the first
light of the morning where ducks study the
revolutionary texts of their shadows stretching
through the water like arteries
the lake is as deep as the Empire State Building is tall
as dark as the Big Apple is
                    bright
          Hinemoana drags men
      into the still water
        her hands shake in the traditional way
            leaving each body to be weighed down by bullion
        soon the eels   begin to feast   black wires bulging

            Hinemoana buys an air fryer   to enjoy her catch
          she was always confused by the phrase
        friend not food
      when obviously   they're foes?

    before going out Hinemoana makes a face mask
    out of the ashes of coral
bits of her start to come away
        morsels tugging free of
          sinew   sliding off   bone

            now fully liquid she is ready to leave
                  her house beneath the sea   gone fishing
                    for more bourgeoisie

Kurangaituku & the Sirens

for Stacey Teague and Whiti Hereaka

Kurangaituku   presses the wind instrument to the side of her   mouth
and blows all twitter and   high-pitched resonance   she's teaching the
others how to play their   parts   u gotta make him think he's got u
they're all following   like synchronised   ghosts   one step out   there
is a   tie-yourself-to-the-mast-of-a-ship quality deep in their awkward
stuttering performance   make men shipwreck   over their own hunger
an ocean   with too much water to drink   alive   drawing swords to
die on a song   Kurangaituku thinks back   to the Te Arawa boy
and his   attempts to melt her wings right off their   bones   can feel a
tightening   getting close to the sun   wasn't something she was invested
in   she wasn't going to fall for all that   not another foolish boy rushing
too fast round the world

Prometheus Collects the Body of His Lover

for Laura Borrowdale

he knocks on the door to a thud
that resonates deep into the rākau
one hand held to his side
he doesn't know what to think
he can't think
his hand hovering over his side
he can't look at anything
he is hurting in far more places than just that
the eagle in the back of his eyelids
all claws and nothing matters now
she answers the door lips pursed
arms folded
he can smell blood
the ghost of his gag reflex tries to remind him –
he swallows
and tries out a smile
practicing it taut over his jaw
she looks past him
and motions to the living room
her black dress moves as if a gentle breeze
hovers around her
a fantail flits from corner
to corner of the room
the only light source
the television
muted

she asks if he wants a coffee

he shakes his head
she goes off into the kitchen anyway
the water already boiling
he is on his knees now next to

the body

Māui looks as if he's just gone to sleep
looks like he dosed off watching *Gone Fishin'*

Prometheus reaches out
his hand hovering over
his lover's chest
there is a plea in his fingers for movement
for the lungs to fill up
for a knock behind his ribs
he rests his hands there and knows the fire has gone out
there is no amount of ahi he could steal
there is no breath but
the whistle of the kettle

she is back in the room now holding two mugs

he asks

can I take him back home?
she looks from the body to him and back again
kāore
she presents the coffee to him
he takes it and notices the warmth
the warmth that could fill a body up
to bursting

they stare at each other
the television light dancing over their bodies
a supermarket deal on schnitzel and rump steak

he takes small sips
black and bitter

there was a Prometheus who would howl at this
would take up patu and strike
a Prometheus who would burn the house down
and leave with the body
and bury him in the rich soils of his kāinga
a Prometheus who would try his hand at succeeding
where Māui had failed
but that wasn't him

not now

he leans over the body
presses nose to nose
a final prayer for te hā
a final attempt to bring him back up from
whatever darkness he'd fallen into

I will take care of him Pomīahi
he belongs here

he nods
knowing he could never follow
he nods
his whole world just hovering over the knock
ringing deep in the rākau

VI

A HEART IN A POT
BOILING OVER

The liver and its strings
all unwound
all tangling
yet they play it
so well, those strings

Echidna & Rona Fucking in the Back Seat of a Car While the Moon Watches

it is dark   and the world is all feeling
the marsupial Moon hungry   for their flesh
but he's getting nothin'   tonight

Echidna and Rona   are pressed against
seatbelt buckles   the cool of the metal   torn seat
covers   foam showing through
Rona is removing their jeans   face concentrating so hard
Echidna snorts *you alright there captain serious*

Rona responds with the finger
Echidna takes the opportunity
and nips her lips around that raised digit
you cheeky shit! and a shudder

they're turning in each other's arms
a jagged whirl of elbows and knees and tails
slumping into exhale

Echidna weighs   her tongue over Rona's
belly   moves with a snake's precision
peels back   lace careful not to rip its gentle
construction   and moves her mouth
over   (*is this okay?* a nod)   a small soft form of flesh

Rona becomes an arc of electricity   hand in Echidna's curls
everything is fogging up in the Moon's light
obscuring his vision   Rona free of that
alabaster pervert   at last

Echidna moves her fingers down
Rona's side   her chipped fingernails
create a squirm

oi!
fuck I'm sorry should have cut them before dyking out

there is a moment made of breath
a wet-steel whistling
into which Echidna winks

Rona just laughs
dyking out what the fuck?

teeth shine in the dark

Echidna & Eve Have a Sleepover

while Echidna curls up onto the couch small
in just the right way   Eve reads poems by
the light of her globe   pours words into the one room unit

what kind of opening up happens here?

the succulents sit   listening intently   as plants do
what music is a tongue   flapping up and down?
the throat holds some strength

Echidna pops a Fruit Burst into her mouth and immediately regrets it
as it clacks into a toothgap   she tries her best to remove it

the poetry lingers

Eve asks Echidna if she's ever seen *Jesus Christ Superstar*
the streetwise Judas   leather jacket intact

Echidna admits she doesn't like musicals
but happens to have it on vinyl and shrugs

when they sleep   they fall asleep
next to the source of all sin
lolly wrappers scattered over the floor

Echidna on The Strand

for Keri Hulme

She sees the crab move in the shallows
this hyperinflection of motion
this hypnotic projection of red
a flame taken and held in exoskeleton
does it grasp the stars with Carcinos grip
does it make a sunset

    she is here to meet someone
    more meat more meat more meat
    have a seat on the dune
    drink from the tips of the swamp
    she is here to meet a monster

    she sees her reflection disperse
    a wave breaking her open

        there is a figure that sits on the other side of the water
        under a tower that spirals up into the clouds
        neither Mr or Mrs thanks
        Echidna understands deep
        what is at stake here

        nothing so alien as being ourselves

Hine-nui-te-pō & the Dominant Species

Hine-nui-te-pō lies down   next to the carpark
a fantail dancing over her fingers   *go* she says
the cars just sit there for hours on end
doing and saying nothing   she watches
as a person approaches   listens to the
short chirp of the vehicle unlocked   what
bird was caught   inside the key
                    Where will this engine
go and what will   it do when it gets there
moving   from one place to
the next   in the most destructive
way   a mammal
grunt in its   non-existent throat
These machines look   like death to her
and she knows   what death looks like.

Echidna & the Spider

for Michelle Rahurahu

the wharepaku disguised by hills in a whitewashed town next to the sea   the
first time in a long time that   Echidna has heard the gulls and smelt the
moana   she's spending time in the big city with its wrong turns and
billboards for   a life well lived   she ain't alone   been travelling with
the Spider   dressed from head to toe in dark denim   Spider's trying out
that goth lifestyle she missed as a kid   mascara for each of her eight   eyes
and that hot tino rangatiratanga look   with the flag taking pride   and place
on her back   *oi Waru Karu you trying to make web in there?* Echidna
cackles   the Spider just shouts   *fuck off* from the stall   *I'm taking a shit*
Echidna settles back swinging her tails   out behind her

////////

Echidna and the Spider both dislike   the same things
and that's enough to love   each other over

pointing at something awful and saying   it is full of awfulness
pulling out their own teeth   and trading them in the dark

Echidna is humming along to a song
that she's had stuck in her head for
years now   can't remember the words
except for   red liquid   red liquid
humming along to silence nothing playing
on the radio
what does it mean wrapped around
such a flat delivery

//////////

they play videogames in the small hours
gamertags in the glow of the multimillion dollar graphical fidelity
talking shit
Ngā Hine-kaitākaro just ripping fake bodies to shreds
in the perfect blooded light of the morning
coloniser after coloniser just getting bullet
after bullet   highscoring in the glaze of the inside
the controller sticky with airplanes   and gummy bears
when a surface clings to the palm   it makes sitting in this violence natural
why would you move   why would you look away?
Echidna relaxing into the crumbed couch
while the Spider does a million things at once
signing *ur all gonna die* with her free hands
the crackle of the speakers   the radical imagination
they both just laugh and laugh

//////////

they're sharing takeaways
next to the ocean
bony butts on a park bench
the Spider signs into the air
did you know liking hot chips makes you gay
Echidna smiles *does it?*
there is just the sound of waves crashing
and the newspaper rustling
the grease making things
transparent

Echidna & a Drag Queen Named Pipi

for Dan Taulapapa McMullin

it's all glitter scales   or light
shifting on a surface   over water   an island made of
photons

how does one undo such acrylics
when they become so attached
not just some faggot in the
kitchen sweeping away the stains of
a dead god

Echidna *dears* Pipi to take her
out   to a bar made of ancestors queerer
than all the motherfucking stars
sisters and dogs   all moving with the tides

sometimes the quiet is all u need to swim in
and sometimes it's the space between words that traps
them wholly

still
with the arms
moves constantly

Prometheus at the Crucifixion

was it a little bit pathetic to feel like flexing on this poor poor man how long
will it last is he timing it Prometheus is sure that Christ can feel it tick through

each failing organ would a loving
Messiah on his way to a fight wit
long lost lover hell is so so hot w
but it feels like it

father really do that to his only son? the
h death Prometheus thinks back to his
as that fire his fault too? it's not quiet
should be Prometheus

recognises the commotion the
ing painful happen to someone
power tells there is nothing but
one word this whole time should
that? Prometheus can see his own
breathing steady despite the worl
of a dying bird the image of you
a pīwakawaka as it falls across the
ever after but Prometheus ain't

boisterous celebration of seeing someth
else someone made evil by a story that
torchlight and sweat Jesus has only said
a son stay so committed to a man like
father in the wound in Christ's side his
d as it is lungs fluttering like the wings
ng Māui pulling on the tail feathers of
threshold eyes popped and flight erratic
here for the end   he's been here before

waiting for a boulder to roll back from a black hole where something should be

VII

ECHIDNA'S FATE

Tungia te ururoa kia tupu whakaritorito te tupu a te harakeke
  she sheds
  her skin
  to grow something
  new

Echidna: Half Woman Half Snake

she lies in the desert her twin tails stretched out   split out underneath her
she travels miles and miles and miles   living off the dust of the land
thanking her great-grandmother for
the food   *oh Papatūānuku how good are thou*   how good
she makes it to the coast   the sun plays with the chop of the wave
she takes to the water to pledge   allegiance to her great-grandfather Tangaroa
a daughter of Tū-te-wehiwehi   he had to have a pākehā name didn't he
Satan? what did he sit on?   she admits she could have misheard   as she
floats nymphal in the
ocean

Echidna Has Breakfast with the Last Moahunter

for Rangi Faith

the ferns are crushed down to the dirt
from frequent travel
there and back

is this where we become ourselves
tallest now
that they have all been eaten?

Echidna just tucks on in
excited for the biggest omelette imaginable

Echidna Thinks about the Future

for Robert Sullivan

she's scratching her eczema   where her tail meets her flesh   the heat's
gotten to her   sweat and raw-red   and dry in a way it shouldn't be in
such humidity   will everything be mostly desert   or sea?   Tangaroa
become all bloated   veins thick with CO_2 will ExxonMobil   one of the
Seven Sisters so sickeningly named   own what is left before taking any
responsibility?   the rich haunting whetū   Elon Musk shit-talking Rehua
the money-hoarding bitch getting hit   a pasty white comet collapsing
into the atmosphere he tried his best to escape   the damage is done
they already took all the knowledge they could   and thoroughly distorted it
whenua for jet-fuel   her people removed from a world of sound   she
thinks   does she want to bring children into a place   like this?   pushes the
star waka out into a sky   where you don't know if what you're looking at   is
stars or satellites

Echidna & the Spider at a Karaoke Bar

they scroll down the list until they get
to the angst   they need   run their throats raw
over   Mr Brightside   and they're calling
A CAB   and they're calling ACABACABACAB   till
both cars collide   8 arms and 2 tails
shaking it in   a pre-sweated room
all of the space is theirs

////////

and they're   in the water   starfish churning
against her scales   and her feet

do they both just want to keep wading until
the whole world   becomes another word for ocean
or another word for afterlife?

but both of them know what comes next
so they turn back around avoiding prickles in the grass
use the doors of the car
to remain decent
while they get changed

////////

sing along to the song of a joke
with the lyrics of laughing
with the spill of the breath
ha ha ha hā hā

Echidna's Fate

for Ava Hofmann

the kuia all dressed in black
standing before an enormous
mouth in the earth
waha all the way down

a tuatara sits eyes lolling
at her feet
the hem of her dress sweeping
over its cold body

the kuia all dressed in black
gestures her come
and all Echidna says before
obliging
before taking those short
shuffling movements
towards the rest of eternity
is *I've never been*,

And with that Echidna is Echidna no more.

Māui Becomes Who S/He Was Meant To Be

after Tāwhanga Nopera's 'Huka can Haka'

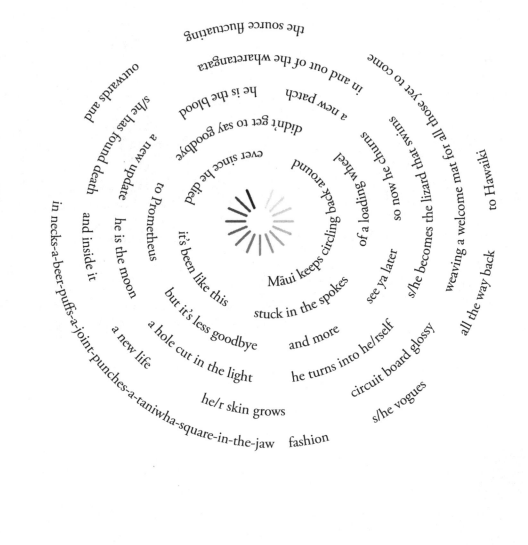

Māui keeps circling back around
ever since he died
it's been like this
but it's less goodbye
and more
stuck in the spokes
of a loading wheel
see ya later
he turns into he/rself
a hole cut in the light
he/r skin grows
fashion
s/he vogues
circuit board glossy
s/he becomes the lizard that swims
in and out of the wharetangata
the source fluctuating
so now he chums
swims
weaving a welcome mat for all those yet to come
all the way back
to Hawaiki
a new life
in necks-a-beer-puffs-a-joint-punches-a-taniwha-square-in-the-jaw
and inside it
he is the moon
to Prometheus
a new update
s/he has found death
and death
outwards and
a new patch
he is the blood
didn't get to say goodbye

Hinenākahirua Repairs Something That Needs Repairing

for Anne-Marie Te Whiu

She sits on her bed in the study slides
                              bead
after bead then quill onto the
                    thread
                         two at a time and then
                    one
                         leaving the parts that are broken to the
                    side
five hollow spines she can feel all the
                         life
               in them leaving.
                         She goes out to the backyard and buries the
                         remnants under juvenile horoeka.
          Over the burial she holds
                    the
          clay from her whenua plays some
                              impotent notes into it and
                    feels free.
                         Afterwards she stands at the table
                    the
                    necklace repaired laid out on its surface
               one
     quill going that way and
               one
               going the other.

NOTES

Many of these poems are intertextually linked to work by other writers. This is a list of where I have drawn from for many of these poems, though a comprehensive list would be impossible as I am influenced in ways I know not.

The rather humorous 'Dramatis Personae' is very much inspired by never angeline north's similar use of the form in *Sea-Witch*.

'The Snake Woman' is influenced by Roma Potiki's 'snake woman came to visit' from her book *Stones in Her Mouth*.

'Echidna Meets Another Eve' & the later poem 'Echidna & Eve Have a Sleepover' are inspired loosely by Aimee-Jane Anderson-O'Connor's work about Eve titled 'Femina'.

'Echidna & Her Bird Tongue' was written in a different form as a gift for Gem Wilder, and is inspired by Ngahuia Te Awekotuku's retelling of the story of Hatupatu and the Bird-woman in her book *Ruahine*.

The 'Echidna & Narcissus' sequence is inspired by jay dodd's work with Narcissus in her book *The Black Condition ft. Narcissus*.

'Echidna Dances w/ Poūkahangatus & All the Colours of the Wind' is inspired by (as is a large part of this book's project) Tayi Tibble's lyric essay 'Poūkahangatus' from her book of the same name.

'Echidna & a Drag Queen Named Pipi' is inspired by Dan Taulapapa McMullin's work in *A Drag Queen Named Pipi*.

'One Must Imagine Sisyphus Is Actually Doing Something Incredibly Important' is something of a continuing conversation between me and Hana Pera Aoake who wrote a response to my first book called *Wailing Waiata* for Compound Press where they compare themselves to Sisyphus.

'Echidna & Nafanua' is inspired by Tusiata Avia's book *Bloodclot* in which she writes automythographically through the figure of the Samoan warrior-goddess Nafanua.

'Echidna Tries Her Best to Console Herculine' is inspired by Aaron Apps' book about Herculine Barbin, *Dear Herculine*.

'Echidna & Hemi in Rānana' is in conversation with the character of James Pōneke from Tina Makereti's novel *The Imaginary Lives of James Pōneke*.

'Echidna Asks Rona One Hundred Questions' is inspired by the work concerning Rona in Reihana Robinson's book *Auē Rona*.

'Kurangaituku & the Sirens' is in conversation with the poem 'Kurangaituku' by Stacey Teague and the book *Kurangaituku* by Whiti Hereaka.

'Hinemoana' is in conversation with four different poems that all share the same name: 'Hinemoana' by Elizabeth Kerekere, Hinemoana Baker, Sinead Overbye and Michelle Rahurahu.

'Echidna on the Strand' is in conversation with Keri Hulme's works *Strands* and *The Bone People*.

'Zoa' is in direct conversation with Joshua Whitehead's *Full-Metal Indigiqueer* whose central figure goes by the name of Zoa.

'Echidna Has Breakfast with the Last Moahunter' is itself in conversation with Rangi Faith's poem 'conversation with a moahunter' from his book of the same name.

ACKNOWLEDGEMENTS

Where these poems had homes before they were bound into this book:

Landfall: 'Echidna: Born of 'Eve & Lucifer', 'Echidna: Half Woman Half Snake', 'Echidna Thinks about the Future', 'Echidna Gets a Name Change', 'Echidna Goes to See the Drone Perform in Front of a Live Audience', 'Kurangaituku & the Sirens'.

Mayhem: 'Echidna Is a Cleaner at Night', 'Mauao & the Angel Michael', 'Tūmatauenga at the Frontlines'.

Poetry NZ Yearbook 2021: 'Hineraukatauri & Her Lover'.

Poetry Shelf: 'Echidna & Nafanua', 'Māui-Pōtiki & Prometheus Make Love', 'Prometheus and His Lover's Great Accomplishment'.

Turbine|Kapohau: 'Zoa', 'Echidna & the Spider', 'Echidna & Narcissus'.

Oscen: 'One Must Imagine Sisyphus is Doing Something Incredibly Important'.

Love in the Time of Covid: 'Hine-nui-te-pō & the Dominant Species'.

Nexus: 'Echidna & Rona Fucking in the Back Seat of a Car While the Moon Watches'.

Scum: 'Echidna Goes Out on the Town; Meets Typhon'.

Thank you to all the editors who believed in these poems especially when they were so obviously a small part of a whole.

First and foremost, Emily. I still don't know the names of dogs.

Michelle Rahurahu, Ruby Solly & Aimee-Jane Anderson-O'Connor, who were the first people to read a version of *Echidna*. Thank you so much for your ongoing support and for the inspiration your writing gives me.

Writers and friends.

Richard, Sharon, Ash & Alex. My family. Ash I'm so excited for your newborn!

Everyone I've forgotten to include that doesn't fit the binary of writer and/or friend.

Nan. I love you.